Mama, Don't Lose Yourself

A positive guide to becoming a mom and loving your child while staying true to yourself.

By
Maggie Dee

1 0
Unidades.

Mama,
Don't Lose
Yourself

A positive guide to becoming a
mom and loving your child while
staying true to yourself.

Maggie Dee

professional before attempting any techniques outlined in this book.

By reading this document, the reader agrees that under no circumstances is the author responsible for any losses, direct or indirect, which are incurred as a result of the use of information contained within this document, including, but not limited to, errors, omissions, or inaccuracies.

Dedication

This book is dedicated to the extraordinary women who wear the title of "Mom" with pride, grace, and unwavering love.

A Note from the Author

Becoming a mother is a life-changing experience that brings immense joy and fulfillment, but it also presents new challenges and responsibilities. Many new moms find themselves struggling to maintain their sense of self while trying to meet the demanding expectations of motherhood.

Mama, Don't Lose Yourself offers ideas on how to balance being a loving, devoted mom without losing sight of who you were before having kids. This book provides practical advice and strategies for staying true to yourself, nurturing your relationships, and finding personal fulfillment beyond your role as a mother.

Together, we'll delve into topics such as acknowledging the challenges of motherhood, rediscovering yourself, navigating relationships, finding fulfillment beyond motherhood, modeling authenticity for your children, and overcoming any guilt and shame.

As a new mom, dog lover, and devoted wife from Vancouver, BC, I have experienced firsthand the struggles and triumphs of motherhood. For the past two years, I have been determined to find a way to love myself and my family equally, without compromising who I am. My commitment to finding balance in motherhood is deeply rooted in the belief that we must "put on our own oxygen masks first" before we can care for others effectively. It is this philosophy that has guided me in writing this book.

There are plenty of cautionary tales out there that focus on the negative aspects of becoming a mom and all too often we're taught that motherhood is one giant state of getting through it at the expense of losing yourself. Instead, I wanted to provide tools and insights that I've discovered in a way to help you live and love your life as both a mother and as an individual.

As you read through the chapters, remember that while you did make the choice to become a mother, you also have the opportunity to continue being yourself while nurturing your child. Motherhood doesn't have to be a battle between your old life and your new one; it can be a harmonious balance that allows you to cherish both aspects of your identity. I'm grateful for your trust and time as we embark on this journey together and learn how to fully embrace the joys of motherhood while remaining true to ourselves.

Table of Contents

Introduction

Are you ready to dive deep into the heart of what it truly means to be a new mom, while still staying true to the person you were before? This book explores the common struggles that moms face as they navigate the complex, rewarding, and sometimes overwhelming journey of motherhood. We'll uncover the challenges of maintaining your sense of self as you step into the role of a caregiver, and how societal expectations can create internal conflict.

Let's dive into the beautiful – and sometimes messy – world of motherhood and self-discovery!

Picture this: you're covered in baby puke, running ragged trying to chase your little one around the house just to get them into the car. You long for a quiet moment to yourself to enjoy a glass of wine or take a nap like you used to do before having kids. Sound familiar? The journey of motherhood is filled with these less-than-glamorous moments that can test your patience and resilience. But don't worry – these are just fleeting moments in time, and they don't have to define you as a woman.

The journey of motherhood is an intricate and multifaceted one, filled with moments of immense joy, love, and growth. However, it also comes with its fair share of challenges, particularly for new mothers who are trying to navigate their new role as caregivers. These challenges can be intensified by societal expectations, personal beliefs, and the desire to maintain one's sense of self. Some of the most common struggles below are ones many new moms face, and they can create internal conflict. If any of these resonate with you, you are not alone!

Identity Shift: One of the most significant challenges new mothers face is the shift in their identity. Becoming a mom means taking on a new role, with new responsibilities and priorities. This change can be disorienting, as it may feel like your previous identity is being replaced by your new one as a mother. You might find yourself wondering who you are outside of your role as a mom and how to maintain your unique qualities and passions.

Time Management: As a new mother, you'll quickly discover that time is a precious commodity.

Between caring for your baby, managing household chores, and trying to maintain a social life, finding time for yourself can seem nearly impossible. This struggle can lead to feelings of being overwhelmed and the fear of losing touch with the things that once brought you joy and fulfillment.

Societal Expectations: Society often places unrealistic expectations on mothers, expecting them to be selfless, devoted caregivers who prioritize their children above all else. This pressure can create internal conflict for new moms who are trying to balance their personal needs with the needs of their child. It can lead to feelings of guilt and shame when mothers take time for themselves or pursue their own interests.

Emotional and Physical Changes: Becoming a mother is accompanied by a myriad of emotional and physical changes. The hormonal fluctuations, physical recovery from childbirth, and the emotional rollercoaster of parenthood can be difficult to navigate. These changes can impact your mood, energy levels, and self-esteem, making it even more challenging to stay connected to your sense of self.

Isolation: Motherhood can be an isolating experience, particularly for new moms who may be adjusting to a new routine and lifestyle. This isolation can make it difficult to maintain existing friendships or create new connections, which can further contribute to feelings of losing oneself.

Remember, while the days may sometimes be long and filled with less-than-glamorous moments, there is immense beauty in the transformation that comes with motherhood. You are not alone in your struggles, and with the right tools and support, you can navigate this new chapter with grace and confidence.

Chapter 1

Acknowledging the Challenges of Motherhood

Countless times I've sat in my armchair, tired eyes fixed on the scattered toys and laundry strewn across the living room. As a mother of a young child, I know the joys of motherhood, but also its immense challenges. I've sighed as my mind fills with thoughts of sleepless nights, tantrums, and endless to-do lists. Yet, amidst the chaos, I've made a conscious effort to acknowledge and embrace the challenges. I know that being a mother means facing uncertainty, self-doubt, and sacrifice, but I also understand that these challenges are part of a journey that will shape my child's life. With a deep breath, I can rise from my chair, ready to face another day with renewed strength and gratitude, knowing that in the midst of the chaos, I'm shaping my child's future with unwavering love and resilience.

Navigating Societal Expectations on Mothers

Let's be honest, societal expectations can have a significant impact on our ability to stay true to ourselves. These expectations often stem from cultural norms, media portrayals, and even well-intentioned advice from friends and family. Unfortunately, these expectations can create pressure and contribute to feelings of guilt or inadequacy when mothers don't meet them or choose to prioritize their own well-being. Let's discuss some common societal expectations placed on mothers and how they can make it challenging to stay true to oneself.

Selflessness: One of the most pervasive societal expectations is that mothers should be completely selfless, prioritizing their children's needs above their own at all times. This notion can make it difficult for mothers to take time for themselves, pursue their interests, or maintain their sense of identity.

Perfection: Society often perpetuates the idea that mothers should be perfect in every aspect, from maintaining a spotless home to effortlessly juggling career and family life. This unrealistic expectation can lead to feelings of guilt and shame when mothers inevitably fall short or struggle in some areas.

Constant Availability: There is a widespread belief that mothers should always be available to their children, regardless of their own needs or desires. This expectation can make it challenging for mothers to set boundaries, take time for self-care, or pursue personal goals outside of their role as a mom.

Traditional Roles: In many cultures, traditional gender roles dictate that mothers should be the primary caregivers and assume most of the household and child-rearing responsibilities. This expectation can create pressure for mothers who wish to share these responsibilities with their partners or pursue careers outside the home.

Unconditional Happiness: Society often romanticizes motherhood, portraying it as a time of unbridled happiness and fulfillment. This expectation can make it difficult for mothers to openly discuss the challenges they face or seek support when they struggle with feelings of sadness, frustration, or being overwhelmed.

These societal expectations can create internal conflict for mothers who are trying to balance their personal needs with the needs of their children. It's crucial to recognize that these expectations are often unrealistic and that it's okay to prioritize yourself and your well-being. By challenging these societal norms and embracing the unique, authentic version of motherhood that works best for you and your family, you can stay true to yourself and foster a healthier, more fulfilling experience as a mom.

Here's a more personal thought! I believe that what we see on social media creates a deceptive impression of reality as a mom. Hey, if you're a go-getter on Instagram and find value in using your spare time to play around on your phone, have at it, but if not, it's one hundred percent okay if you're not coming up with your own genius ways to entertain your toddler or making Reels of your kids playing in the sand. Old-fashioned toys are just fine and nor will your child ask you why they don't have these Reels made of them. Also, no one – and I mean not a single soul – is sitting there waiting for you to post something of your child. So, if you can't find the balance, then put your phone down (or better yet, delete the app) and start enjoying the fulfillment of literally just watching your child learn and have fun. Those memories will stay with you forever. And your inner self will thank you! In life and motherhood, no matter how you do it, there will always be someone who will judge or think they can do it better, so don't worry about what people think and just do you.

Overcoming Physical, Emotional, and Mental Challenges

New mothers face a variety of challenges as they adjust to their new role. These challenges can significantly impact one's sense of self, making it difficult to maintain a strong sense of identity and self-worth. Let's explore some of these challenges and how they can affect a new mother's sense of self.

Physical Challenges: The physical changes that accompany pregnancy and childbirth can be demanding on a woman's body. Recovery from childbirth, adjusting to breastfeeding, and coping with sleep deprivation take a toll on a new mother's energy levels and self-image. These physical challenges can make it difficult for new mothers to feel confident and connected to their pre-pregnancy selves.

Emotional Challenges: New mothers often experience a wide range of emotions, from the joy and love they feel for their newborn to feelings of anxiety, sadness, or even depression. Hormonal changes, coupled with the stress of adjusting to new responsibilities, can contribute to emotional instability.

These emotional challenges can make it difficult for new mothers to feel in control of their emotions and maintain a strong sense of self.

Mental Challenges: The mental challenges new mothers face can be just as significant as the physical and emotional ones. The constant decision-making, problem-solving, and multitasking that come with motherhood can be mentally exhausting. Additionally, new mothers often feel overwhelmed by the sheer amount of new information they need to process and the high stakes of their choices. These mental challenges can make it difficult for new mothers to feel confident in their abilities and maintain a clear sense of self.

Unleashing Your Inner Strength in Motherhood

You are stronger than you know, and it's time to tap into that hidden strength that lies within each and every one of us! As you embark on the incredible journey of motherhood, remember that you are not alone, and you are more than capable of overcoming any challenges that may come your way. With an upbeat, positive attitude, let's explore how to uncover and harness this inner strength, allowing you to flourish as a mother and as an individual.

First, believe in yourself and trust your instincts. As a mother, you possess a unique intuition that can guide you through the toughest decisions and challenges. Embrace this inner wisdom, and have faith in your ability to make the best choices for you and your family.

Next, practice self-compassion and self-love. Motherhood can be tough, and it's essential to be kind to yourself during this transformative journey. Celebrate your victories, no matter how small, and remember to forgive yourself for any perceived shortcomings. You are doing your best, and that is more than enough.

Stay connected with your support network. Surround yourself with positive, uplifting people who encourage and support you on your journey. Having a strong network of friends, family, and fellow mothers can make a world of difference in helping you tap into your inner strength.

Make time for self-care and personal growth. Nurturing your own needs and interests is essential to maintaining your sense of self and fostering your inner strength. Set aside time to engage in activities that bring you joy, relaxation, and a sense of accomplishment. As you invest in yourself, you'll find that your inner strength grows in tandem.

Finally, embrace the journey and all its ups and downs. Motherhood is a wild ride, filled with laughter, tears, triumphs, and setbacks. By embracing each moment and learning from your experiences, you'll cultivate resilience and the ability to adapt and grow.

When you find yourself in the thick of a "I can't continue like this" moment, try to remember that this is just life now, a fleeting moment in time. Three, ten, maybe fifteen years from now, you'll look back and wonder where it went and laugh at all the good and bad times. If you have a partner, remember to lean on them during these moments and have a giggle knowing you're in this together and you're definitely not the first or last parents to go through a public tantrum.

As you uncover your hidden strength and tap into it, you'll find yourself thriving in your new role as a mother. With an upbeat and encouraging spirit, you'll forge a path through motherhood that not only nurtures your child but also allows you to flourish as a strong, confident, and authentic individual. So, let's embrace this beautiful journey together and celebrate the incredible strength that lies within each of us!

Mastering Self-Reflection, Self-Care, and Supportive Environments

To flourish as both mothers and individuals, it's essential to prioritize self-reflection, self-care, and creating a supportive environment. Here are some strategies to help you achieve this balance:

Self-reflection:

- Keep a journal: Writing about your experiences, thoughts, and feelings can help you process emotions, identify patterns, and gain insights into your personal growth.

- Set aside quiet time: Carve out moments in your day for quiet reflection and meditation, which can help you stay grounded and connected to your inner self.

- Seek feedback: Don't be afraid to ask for feedback from trusted friends, family members, or even a therapist. They can provide valuable insight and a fresh perspective.

Self-care:

- Schedule "me time": Dedicate time in your schedule for activities that nurture your mind, body, and soul. This can include exercise, hobbies, or simply relaxing with a good book.

- Prioritize sleep: Getting enough rest is crucial for your physical and mental well-being. Make sleep a priority and establish a bedtime routine that promotes relaxation for both you and your child. After all, if they sleep, you sleep!

- Establish a good routine that works for you. This could look like one hour of housework after your child goes to bed, and then it's time to watch TV.

- Eat well and stay hydrated: Nourish your body with a balanced diet and drink plenty of water to maintain your energy levels and overall health.

Create a supportive environment:

- Build a strong support network: Connect with friends, family, and fellow mothers who can offer encouragement, advice, and emotional support.

- Set boundaries: Clearly communicate your needs and limits to others, and don't be afraid to say no when necessary. Establishing boundaries can help you maintain a healthy balance between your personal and parenting life.

- Delegate and ask for help: Share responsibilities with your partner or other family members, and ask for help when needed. Remember that you don't have to do everything on your own.

Personal growth:

- Set realistic goals: Identify areas in your life where you want to grow and set achievable, measurable goals to help you stay focused and motivated.

- Embrace lifelong learning: Keep your mind engaged and stimulated by reading, attending workshops, or taking courses in areas of interest.

- Practice gratitude: Cultivate a grateful mindset by regularly acknowledging the positive aspects of your life. This can help you maintain an optimistic outlook and enhance overall well-being.

Are you like Sarah?

As Sarah sat on the couch, exhausted from a day filled with diapers, feedings, and endless household chores, she couldn't help but feel as if she was losing herself. It seemed as if her entire life now revolved around taking care of her baby, and she struggled to remember who she was before becoming a mother.

One day, while scrolling through her TV channels, Sarah came across an inspiring story of a woman who had managed to find a balance between being a devoted mother and staying true to herself. This woman had faced similar challenges as Sarah, but instead of letting her identity be swallowed up by motherhood, she had discovered ways to reclaim her sense of self and still be an amazing mom. She reported that new mothers feel a loss of their pre-motherhood identity, and most, if not all of them reported that self-care is a key component to overcoming this struggle. This uplifting example shows that it is possible for new moms to find balance and maintain their sense of self while still being devoted caregivers. Sarah realized she needed to make a change, and this was the inspiration she needed to start her journey towards finding that balance. With determination and support, Sarah, like many other new moms, can rediscover their identities and thrive in both motherhood and their personal lives.

Key Takeaways:

- Societal expectations can place immense pressure on mothers, making it difficult for them to stay true to themselves.
- New mothers face numerous physical, emotional, and mental challenges that can affect their sense of self.
- By acknowledging these challenges, mothers can begin to understand the importance of finding a balance between motherhood and personal identity.
- Strategies such as self-reflection, self-care, and creating a supportive environment can help mothers to flourish both as individuals and caregivers.

Chapter 2

Rediscovering Yourself After Motherhood

The Struggle Is Real! One day you're a fit, energy-filled, hardworking woman who loves to socialize and entertain, and the next day you're a tired, mentally-weighed down mom, whose morning was filled with making lunches and carting kids off to school only to come home and clean up the mess that still fills your home from the previous night's shenanigans. Your hair is loosely tied up in a bun, your clothes have tears in them, and you're sitting there wondering, how are you supposed to feel like the woman you were before?

The Journey of Rediscovering Yourself after Motherhood

The journey of rediscovering yourself after motherhood is a deeply personal and transformative experience. It often involves a mix of self-reflection, goal-setting, and embracing change as you navigate the new territory of being both a mother and an individual with your own passions, interests, and aspirations. While every mother's journey is different, there are a few of the same key steps.

Embrace the Transformation

Becoming a mother is undoubtedly one of the most profound life changes you will ever experience. As you embark on this new journey, it's essential to understand that you are not the same person you were before, and that's perfectly okay. In fact, it's an opportunity for growth, self-discovery, and personal evolution. Let's take a closer look at some key aspects to consider as you embrace the transformation.

Accepting Change

As a new mother, you'll encounter numerous changes in your daily routine, your relationships, and your priorities. It's important to accept and adapt to these changes with an open mind and a flexible attitude. Understand that change is a natural part of life, and it's what helps us grow and develop as individuals.

You might find that your daily schedule has been turned upside down, or that you're no longer able to participate in certain activities as much as you used to. It's essential to be patient with yourself and recognize that it's normal to feel a bit overwhelmed at first. As you become more comfortable in your new role, you'll learn to navigate these changes with grace and resilience.

Maintaining Your Core Values and Passions

While many aspects of your life will change, your core values and passions can remain intact. These are the building blocks of your identity and should continue to guide your decisions and actions. Make a conscious effort to stay true to your values and passions, and integrate them into your new life as a mother.

For example, if you've always been passionate about fitness, find creative ways to incorporate exercise into your routine, like taking your baby for a walk or trying a mommy-and-me yoga class. If you value creativity, set aside time for painting, writing, or any other artistic pursuit that brings you joy. By staying connected to even the littlest of things that matter most to you, you'll continue to nurture your sense of self.

Giving Yourself Permission to Grow

Growth and personal development are essential components of a fulfilling life. Embrace the new challenges and experiences that come with motherhood as opportunities for personal growth. Give yourself permission to learn from your mistakes, to adapt and evolve, and to become the best version of yourself.

Remember that no one is perfect, and that it's okay to stumble along the way. Motherhood is a journey, not a destination, and you'll continue to grow and change as both a mother and an individual. By embracing this transformation with an open heart and a positive attitude, you'll be well on your way to rediscovering yourself after motherhood.

Self-Reflection

Take the time to reflect on your life before motherhood and identify the activities, interests, and values that made you feel fulfilled and happy.

By taking a step back and looking inward, you can gain clarity on what truly matters to you and what brings you happiness. Let's delve into some tips and techniques for practicing self-reflection effectively.

Reflecting on Your Pre-Motherhood Life

Begin by reminiscing about your life before becoming a mom. Think about the activities, interests, and values that made you feel fulfilled and happy. Did you enjoy spending time outdoors, engaging in creative pursuits, or connecting with friends and family? By revisiting these memories, you can rediscover the aspects of your life that truly spark joy and satisfaction.

Keeping a Journal

Consider keeping a journal to document your thoughts and feelings during your self-reflection process. Writing about your experiences can help you gain a better understanding of your priorities and desires. It also serves as a safe space to express your emotions, concerns, and aspirations without judgment.

Set aside some quiet time each day or week to write in your journal. You can write freely about your thoughts, feelings, and memories, or you can use specific prompts to guide your writing. For example, ask yourself questions like, "What activities brought me joy before becoming a mom?" or "How can I integrate my passions into my new life as a mother?" Reflecting on these questions will help you identify the aspects of your life that you want to nurture and prioritize moving forward.

<u>Embracing Change and Growth</u>

As you engage in self-reflection, you may notice that some of your interests and priorities have shifted since becoming a mom. This is a natural part of the journey, and it's essential to embrace these changes with an open heart. Recognize that it's okay to let go of certain aspects of your pre-motherhood life if they no longer serve you or align with your current values.

At the same time, remain open to discovering new passions and interests that may have emerged as a result of your experiences as a mother. By staying true to yourself and allowing room for growth and change, you can continue to evolve as both a mom and an individual.

Remember, the process of self-reflection is an ongoing journey. By regularly checking in with yourself and taking the time to nurture your passions and values, you'll be able to maintain a strong sense of self as you navigate the beautiful, complex world of motherhood.

Reconnecting with your Passions and Hobbies

Once you've identified the activities and interests that were important to you before becoming a mother, try to reintegrate them into your life. Here are some ways to reconnect with your interests and hobbies while balancing your new role as a mother:

Schedule Dedicated Time for Yourself

One of the most effective ways to ensure you're prioritizing your hobbies and passions is to set aside dedicated time for them in your weekly schedule. It may seem challenging initially, especially with the demands of motherhood, but carving out even just a small window of time can make a significant difference in your overall happiness and well-being.

Try to identify periods during the week when you can focus on your interests, even if it's just for thirty minutes or an hour. You might consider arranging for childcare, swapping babysitting duties with a friend, or using your child's nap time as an opportunity to engage in your favorite activities. By creating a consistent routine, you'll be more likely to commit to nurturing your passions.

Join Clubs, Groups, or Classes

Connecting with others who share your interests can be a powerful motivator to pursue your hobbies and passions. These gatherings offer a fantastic opportunity to socialize, learn, and grow while also providing you with a built-in support network of like-minded individuals.

Participating in such groups can also be a great way to make new friends, particularly if they're also moms who can relate to your experiences and challenges. Together, you can encourage one another to stay true to yourselves while navigating the joys and struggles of motherhood.

Be Flexible

As a new mom, it's important to recognize that your interests and hobbies may need to evolve to fit your current lifestyle. Be open to adapting your passions in ways that make them more accessible and manageable as a mother. For example, if you used to enjoy painting large canvases, consider exploring smaller-scale art projects that can be more easily completed during your limited free time.

Alternatively, you might explore hobbies that can be enjoyed alongside your child or can be easily picked up and put down as needed. By being flexible and creative, you can continue to pursue your passions while also embracing your new role as a mom. For example, if you used to enjoy baking from scratch in your spare time but it takes too long now, consider baking from a premade mix. Its quicker and may offer you the same feeling of enjoyment waiting for your home to fill up with the scent of a baked good.

By committing to reconnecting with your passions, you'll not only feel more fulfilled, but you'll also be setting a positive example for your child, demonstrating the importance of self-care and personal growth.

Prioritizing Self-Care

Self-care is essential for maintaining your physical, emotional, and mental well-being. Develop a self-care routine that allows you to recharge and reconnect with yourself. This could include activities like exercise, meditation, spending time in nature, or simply going to get your nails done.

Taking care of yourself is an essential part of being a mother, and it's crucial not to neglect your own needs. By prioritizing self-care, you'll be better equipped to face the challenges of motherhood while staying true to yourself. Let's explore some ways to create a self-care routine that helps you recharge and reconnect with yourself:

Choose Activities that Nourish Your Body and Mind

Self-care isn't a one-size-fits-all approach. We all have our own activities that make us feel relaxed, rejuvenated, and connected to ourselves. Experiment with different activities to find what works best for you, and remember that self-care should be enjoyable and fulfilling.

Set realistic expectations

While it's important to prioritize self-care, remember that it's okay to be flexible and adapt your routine as needed. Some days, you may only have a few minutes to spare, while on others, you might have more time to indulge. Focus on making the most of the time you have and being gentle with yourself if you're unable to meet your self-care goals every day.

Create a Supportive Environment

Enlist the help of your partner, family members, or friends to create a supportive environment that allows you to prioritize self-care. Communicate your needs and let them know how they can help, whether it's by taking over childcare duties for a short period, joining you in your self-care activities, or simply offering a listening ear when you need to talk.

Remember that Self-Care Benefits Everyone

Prioritizing your own well-being isn't selfish—it's essential for your overall health and happiness. By taking care of yourself, you'll be better equipped to care for your family and be a more present, engaged, and authentic parent. Plus, modeling the importance of self-care to your children sets a positive example for their own self-care habits as they grow.

Be patient with yourself and recognize that your body has changed and that's okay. It won't happen overnight, but with a little patience, self-love and acceptance, you will be you again. Sure, you might have more grey hairs and wrinkles and your boobs fall flat after nursing every two hours for a year straight, but then again, so do most moms'. And bringing a mini you into this world far surpasses any of this. It may not appear so at first, but taking baby steps – no pun intended – towards regaining yourself identity will lead to a much more relaxed, less stressed mom. Again, do whatever it is that works for you. A fifteen-minute yoga session, an hour-long walk alone, or a trip to the mall. Whatever it is that makes you happy, take that time for yourself and before you know it, you'll soon begin to recognize the woman in the mirror as the same person you were before motherhood.

Seeking Support

Motherhood can be an incredible and fulfilling experience, but it can also be challenging and, at times, isolating. Connecting with others who understand your journey can provide valuable insights, encouragement, and camaraderie. Building a support network of fellow moms and others who can empathize with your experiences can make a significant difference in your overall well-being. Let's explore some ways to seek support as you rediscover yourself after motherhood:

Join a Local Parenting Group

Local parenting groups can be a fantastic way to connect with other moms in your community. These groups often organize playdates, meet-ups, and other social events, allowing you to bond with fellow parents and share your experiences. You might find lifelong friends or even mentors who can provide guidance and support as you navigate motherhood.

Participate in Online Communities

The internet has made it easier than ever to connect with others who share similar interests, experiences, and challenges. Join online forums or social media groups focused on motherhood, self-discovery, and personal growth. These virtual communities can offer advice, support, and camaraderie from the comfort of your own home. Plus, you'll have the opportunity to learn from moms around the world, broadening your perspectives on motherhood and self-discovery.

Attend Workshops and Seminars

Workshops and seminars focused on self-discovery, personal growth, and parenting can provide valuable insights and tools to help you navigate your journey. These events often feature expert speakers and interactive sessions, giving you the opportunity to learn from professionals in the field and engage with fellow attendees. Additionally, attending workshops and seminars can help you stay informed about the latest research, trends, and strategies related to motherhood and self-development.

Reach Out to Friends and Family

Your existing network of friends and family members can be an invaluable source of support as you rediscover yourself after motherhood. Don't be afraid to reach out and share your experiences, challenges, and successes with your loved ones. They might be able to offer guidance, encouragement, or even just a listening ear when you need it most.

Sometimes the best way to rediscover the old self is to engage with old friends. Carve out time for friends who may or may not have kids and who you used to connect with prior to having your own children. A little bit of quality time with that person can quickly remind you of who you were and can still be.

Consider Professional Support

If you find yourself struggling to cope with the challenges of motherhood or rediscovering your sense of self, it might be helpful to seek professional support. A therapist or counselor can offer guidance, tools, and techniques to help you navigate this journey with greater ease and confidence. Remember, asking for help is a sign of strength, not weakness. Remember, dear reader, you are not alone!

Setting Goals

As you embark on the journey of rediscovering your identity after motherhood, setting clear, realistic goals is an essential step. Goals give you a sense of direction and purpose, and they can help you stay focused and motivated as you work toward becoming the best version of yourself. Here's how you can effectively set and achieve your goals:

Be Specific and Realistic

When setting goals, it's important to be specific and realistic about what you want to achieve. Instead of setting vague goals like "be happier" or "find a hobby," focus on more concrete objectives, such as "practice yoga three times a week" or "learn how to knit." Being specific will give you a clearer idea of what you need to do to accomplish your goals and make you feel better by leaps and bounds.

Break Down Your Goals

Once you have a clear idea of what you want to achieve, break down your goals into smaller, manageable steps. This will make it easier to stay focused and motivated, as you'll be able to see your progress and celebrate small victories along the way. For example, if your goal is to read more books, start by setting a goal to read one chapter per night and gradually increase the frequency as you become more comfortable with your reading routine.

Prioritize Your Goals

Take some time to reflect on which goals align best with your values and passions, and prioritize them accordingly. Remember that it's okay to adjust your priorities as you grow and evolve.

Set Deadlines and Track Your Progress

Assigning deadlines to your goals can help you stay focused and maintain a sense of urgency. Track your progress by keeping a journal or using goal-setting apps, and make adjustments as needed. Regularly reviewing your progress can be a great motivator, as it allows you to see how far you've come and helps you celebrate your achievements.

<u>Stay Flexible and Adaptable</u>

Life as a mother can be unpredictable, so it's important to stay flexible and adaptable when working toward your goals. Be prepared to adjust your plans or modify your goals as needed, and don't be too hard on yourself if you encounter setbacks or obstacles. If you and your partner had plans to celebrate a friend's birthday and your toddler falls ill so you have to stay home, remind yourself that yes, it's disappointing, but there will be others. Remember, the journey of rediscovery is a process, and it's okay if things don't go exactly as planned.

Embracing Balance

Finding balance between your role as a mother and your personal identity is crucial to maintaining your sense of self. It's essential to understand that you can be both a devoted mother and a fulfilled individual. Here's how you can work towards creating a harmonious balance that allows you to nurture both your child and yourself:

Prioritize Your Time

Time management can be key when it comes to finding balance in your life. Begin by setting priorities and creating a schedule that allows you to devote time to your child, your personal interests, and your self-care routine. Be realistic about your time constraints, and be flexible enough to adjust your schedule when needed.

Communicate with Your Partner

Discuss your needs and expectations, and work together to create a supportive environment where both of you can thrive. Sharing responsibilities and making time for each other can help strengthen your relationship and create a more balanced family dynamic.

Set Boundaries

Try setting boundaries as it can be an important aspect for maintaining balance. Be clear about your limits and communicate them to others. This could mean setting boundaries with your partner, family members, or friends when it comes to your time, energy, and personal space. Remember that it's okay to say no and prioritize your well-being.

<u>Be Present</u>

When you're spending time with your child or focusing on your personal interests, try to be fully present. Avoid multitasking or constantly thinking about other responsibilities. Being present allows you to fully engage in and enjoy each activity, which can contribute to a greater sense of balance and fulfillment.

<u>Be Patient with Yourself</u>

Finding balance is a journey, and it's important to be patient with yourself as you navigate this process. Understand that it may take time to strike the perfect balance, and don't be too hard on yourself if things don't fall into place immediately. Embrace the process and celebrate your progress along the way.

Are you like Emily?

Emily was passionate about photography. Prior to having children, she would grab her camera on the weekends and head into the country to capture beautiful landscapes and wildlife. After becoming a mother, she began to feel as though she was losing touch with her creative side. Her life seemed to revolve around her children, and she found it increasingly difficult to prioritize herself and her interests.

One day, Emily came across a study that resonated with her deeply. The study found that mothers who prioritize self-care and personal growth have a positive impact on their children's well-being and development. The researchers discovered that these mothers were more likely to raise children with higher levels of self-esteem, emotional intelligence, and resilience.

This revelation sparked a fire within Emily. One day she picked up her camera and headed into the country to capture images of some beautiful horses on a farm. The time spent alone and the fresh country air reignited her love of photography, making her realize that by taking the time to rediscover herself and focusing on her own well-being, she would not only be happier but also be a better mother to her children. Emily made time for her hobby, picking up her camera on the weekends or whenever she had a spare minute and marveled at how much better she felt just by making beautiful pictures again.

As Emily once again embraced her hobby, her life began to transform. She felt more confident, energized, and fulfilled than ever before. And, as the study had suggested, her children began to thrive as well. They developed a stronger sense of self-worth and resilience, inspired by their mother's dedication to personal growth and authenticity.

Key Takeaways:

- Rediscovering yourself after motherhood is crucial for maintaining your sense of self and well-being.

- Identifying your passions, values, and goals can help you create a more fulfilling and balanced life.

- Prioritizing self-care and personal growth positively impacts both your own happiness and your children's development.

- Seeking support and nurturing meaningful relationships can enhance your journey of self-discovery.

- Embracing the balance between your role as a mother and your personal identity is essential for living an authentic, joyful life.

Chapter 3

Navigating Relationships

Are you struggling to navigate the intricate web of relationships in your life after becoming a mom? From late-night conversations with friends to cozy date nights with your partner, it can feel like everything has been turned upside down. But don't worry; we're here to help you find your way back to meaningful connections.

In this chapter, we'll dive into the challenges of maintaining relationships with friends, family, and your partner as you navigate the whirlwind of motherhood. From setting boundaries to communicating effectively, we'll provide you with the strategies you need to strengthen your connections and build a solid support network. So, let's begin this journey together and rediscover the joys of nurturing relationships, even when you're juggling diaper changes and your baby's unpredictable sleep schedule.

Navigating Relationship Challenges

The journey into motherhood brings with it a plethora of changes, both within ourselves and in our relationships with others. Maintaining relationships with friends, family, and a partner after becoming a mother can be quite a challenge. Below are some of the common obstacles that new moms face:

Shift in Priorities and Interests: As a new mom, your focus shifts to your baby and their needs. This change in priorities might make it difficult to connect with friends who aren't parents or to find common ground with family members. Moreover, the time and energy you used to invest in these relationships may now be limited, which can create a sense of distance.

Lack of Time and Energy: The demands of motherhood often leave new moms feeling exhausted and overwhelmed. With a baby to care for, household chores to manage, and possibly work responsibilities to juggle, finding time to nurture relationships can be quite challenging.

Changing Dynamics with Your Partner: The addition of a new family member can change the dynamics between you and your partner. Sleepless nights, parenting disagreements, and the division of household responsibilities can put a strain on your relationship, making it challenging to maintain a strong connection.

Setting Boundaries: With a new baby, it's crucial to set boundaries with friends and family members to protect your well-being and the well-being of your child. This process can be difficult, as it may require you to have tough conversations with loved ones.

Acknowledging these challenges is the first step towards finding solutions to maintain and strengthen your relationships with friends, family, and your partner after becoming a mother.

Effective Boundaries and Communication with Loved Ones

Setting boundaries and communicating effectively with loved ones are essential skills for new moms as they navigate the challenges of motherhood and deal with what I like to call "messy mom moments". Here are some strategies and examples "messy mom moments" to help you establish boundaries and improve communication with your friends, family, and partner:

Be Clear and Assertive: Clearly express your boundaries and expectations to your loved ones. For example, if you're struggling with sleep deprivation and need some quiet time, let your friends and family know that you prefer not to receive visitors during certain hours. Being assertive about your needs can help prevent misunderstandings and ensure that your boundaries are respected.

Messy Mom Moment: Your in-laws drop by unexpectedly during your baby's nap time, making it difficult for your little one to sleep. Instead of letting your frustration build up, calmly explain your baby's sleep schedule and politely ask them to visit during designated hours.

Practice Active Listening: When communicating with your loved ones, try to actively listen to their concerns and feelings. This can help you better understand their perspective and foster a more open and supportive dialogue.

Messy Mom Moment: Your partner expresses frustration about feeling left out of parenting decisions. Instead of getting defensive, listen to their concerns and work together to find ways to include them more in the decision-making process.

Choose the Right Time and Place: When discussing sensitive topics or setting boundaries, choose a time and place where you can have a calm and focused conversation. Avoid discussing important matters when you're feeling overwhelmed or emotional.

Messy Mom Moment: You're at a family gathering, and your sister-in-law keeps offering unsolicited parenting advice. Instead of confronting her in front of everyone, wait for a more private moment to discuss your feelings and set boundaries.

Use "I" statements: When expressing your feelings and needs, use "I" statements to avoid sounding accusatory or confrontational. This approach can make it easier for your loved ones to understand your perspective and respond empathetically.

Messy Mom Moment: Your friend keeps canceling plans at the last minute, leaving you feeling disappointed and frustrated. Instead of accusing them of being unreliable, say, "I feel hurt when our plans get canceled last minute. I'd appreciate it if we could find a more consistent time to catch up."

Offer Solutions: When setting boundaries or addressing concerns, try to offer solutions or compromises that can help maintain a healthy and balanced relationship with your loved ones.

Messy Mom Moment: Your parents want to visit more often than you're comfortable with. Instead of flat-out refusing, suggest a visitation schedule that works for both parties, or propose video calls as an alternative to in-person visits.

By applying these strategies, you can effectively communicate your needs and boundaries while maintaining positive relationships with your loved ones during this transformative period of motherhood.

Rekindling the Connection with Your Partner

After becoming a mother, the romantic relationship with your partner can often feel like it's been pushed to the back-burner. Between the constant demands of caring for a new baby, sleepless nights, and tackling never-ending household chores, finding the energy or desire for romance might seem impossible. Let's face it – feeling sexy when you're exhausted, covered in spit-up, wearing a nursing bra, and struggling to recall the last time you showered is no easy feat. But even amidst the chaos of motherhood, it's crucial to invest time and effort into nurturing your relationship. A strong partnership provides emotional support, fosters better communication, and creates a more harmonious environment for both you and your child.

I get it – rekindling that romantic spark isn't always a walk in the park when you're juggling the responsibilities of being a mom. The reality is that parenthood is messy, and finding the time and energy for intimacy can be challenging. But that doesn't mean it's impossible! It's all about embracing the imperfections, finding humor in the chaos, and remembering that your relationship is still a priority, even when it might not feel like it.

In the midst of those unglamorous, "real talk" moments, try to remind yourself that your partner is going through this journey with you. They've seen you at your best and your worst, and they're still by your side. It's essential to maintain that emotional connection, even when life gets messy. Share your thoughts, feelings, and fears with one another, and remember that you're a team.

As you navigate the challenges of parenthood together, keep in mind that the romance doesn't have to disappear entirely. Get creative with date nights, whether it's a candlelit dinner at home after the baby is asleep or a simple walk around the neighborhood. Find joy in those small, stolen moments, like a quick hug or a whispered "I love you" in the middle of a diaper change.

Here are some strategies to help you reconnect with your partner and strengthen your relationship:

Schedule Regular Date Nights: Set aside time for just the two of you, even if it's just an hour or two every week or every other week. Use this time to focus on each other and enjoy shared activities, whether it's going out for dinner, watching a movie, or taking a walk together. Commit to this time. Hire a sitter or trade with another parent.

"Babysitting clubs" can be an amazing way to take turns having all the kids over at one house each week while the other parents go out for a few hours. Rely on that network you've curated and ask them to support you – they'll jump at the chance to help out.

Communicate Openly and Honestly: Make a conscious effort to discuss your feelings, concerns, and needs with your partner. Maintaining open lines of communication will help you both understand and support each other better as you navigate the challenges of parenthood. Schedule quick coffee dates in the kitchen to check-in with one another. Stay vulnerable and don't be afraid to ask for what you need. Moms are so capable and look like they have it all together, so your partner might not even realize that you're missing time with them.

Be Affectionate: Small gestures of affection – such as hugging, holding hands, or leaving a sweet lunchbox note – can go a long way in keeping the emotional connection strong. Make it a point to express your love and appreciation for each other regularly. Remember to use the strategies that got you pregnant in the first place! You already know what turns your partner on, whether it's a strip tease, a bubble bath with candles, or a candlelit dinner. Similarly, they know what you like. Remind one another how sexy and spontaneous you can be.

Share Parenting Responsibilities: Work together as a team to care for your child and manage household tasks. This will not only ease the burden on both of you but also create a sense of partnership and shared purpose in your relationship.

<u>Be Patient and Understanding</u>: Parenthood is a challenging and transformative experience for both partners. Recognize that you're both learning and growing, and extend patience and understanding to each other as you adapt to your new roles and responsibilities. There are lots of different ways to parent, and you might each have different methods and strengths. Acknowledge your partner's strengths and remind each other that you're both just trying your best. This is an adventure you're on together.

<u>Seek Professional Help if Needed</u>: If you find that your relationship is struggling despite your best efforts, consider seeking the guidance of a couple's therapist or counselor to help you navigate the challenges and rebuild your connection. This is common, so don't feel like a failure if you can't figure it out together and need some tips and tricks from a professional counselor. They've seen it all before and would welcome the opportunity to help you and your partner solve any parenting challenges to ensure that your relationship stays strong.

Remember that maintaining a strong, loving relationship with your partner is an essential aspect of your overall well-being and happiness as a mother. By investing time and effort into rekindling your connection, you'll create a more harmonious and supportive environment for your entire family.

Are you like Clara?

She had always been an outgoing and independent person with a wide circle of friends and a loving partner. After giving birth to her daughter, Clara found herself struggling to maintain her relationships, as her focus was primarily on her new baby. She noticed that her friendships were drifting apart, her connection with her partner was strained, and she felt lonely and isolated.

Clara, like many others, was part of this majority. One day, she read a book that discussed the challenges faced by new moms and the importance of maintaining a support network. Inspired by the stories and strategies, she decided to take action.

She tried to reconnect with her friends, both parents and non-parents, and she started setting boundaries and communicating more openly with her loved ones. Gradually, she rebuilt her support network and found her relationships flourishing once again.

Key Takeaways:

- Becoming a mother can impact your relationships with friends, family, and your partner, leading to feelings of isolation and loneliness.

- Setting boundaries and communicating effectively are essential strategies for maintaining healthy relationships with your loved ones.

- Building a diverse support network that includes fellow parents and non-parents can help you manage stress, share experiences, and maintain a sense of balance in your life.

Chapter 4

Finding Fulfillment Beyond Motherhood

Are you ready to explore your passions and dreams beyond your role as a mother? As fulfilling as motherhood can be, it's essential to recognize and honor the other facets of your identity. In this chapter, we'll dive into the exciting journey of finding purpose, passion, and fulfillment beyond your role as a mom.

Let's face it, it's all too easy to get swept up in the whirlwind of diaper changes, playdates, and bedtime routines, leaving little time or energy for anything else. But what about that pottery class you've always wanted to take, the career goals you've put on hold, or the social activities that used to bring you joy? Your life as a mom is only one part of who you are, and nurturing your interests and aspirations is key to achieving a sense of balance and happiness.

So, let's embark on this exciting journey together and discover how to find fulfillment beyond motherhood – even when you're juggling a fussy baby, a sink full of dishes, and a never-ending to-do list. Because when you honor and pursue your passions, you become an even more amazing mom, role model, and person.

More than a Mother

Discovering fulfillment and purpose beyond your role as a mother is crucial for achieving a well-rounded sense of balance and well-being in life. By investing time and energy into nurturing your individual interests, passions, and goals, you not only empower yourself as a person but also create a deeper connection with your authentic self. Embracing your personal aspirations helps you maintain your identity while still embracing your role as a mom, leading to a more satisfying and rewarding life experience. Moreover, pursuing personal growth outside of motherhood can enhance your overall happiness and mental health, making you an even better parent in the long run.

Practical Tips for Pursuing Career Goals and Personal Passions

Pursuing career goals or personal passions can be challenging. With the demands of childcare, household responsibilities, and the physical and emotional challenges that come with motherhood, it's easy to feel overwhelmed or as if there's no time left for your own ambitions. However, carving out space for your professional aspirations and personal interests is essential for maintaining a sense of balance and fulfillment in your life.

Here are some practical tips for pursuing your career goals or personal passions:

Set Specific, Achievable Goals: Clearly define your career or personal goals and break them down into smaller, manageable steps. This will help you maintain focus and track your progress over time.

Prioritize Your Time: Assess your daily schedule and identify areas where you can allocate time to work on your goals or passions. Prioritize these activities and make them non-negotiable in your routine. This could mean setting aside a few hours each week for your hobby or dedicating one evening per week to work on a personal project. Creating a schedule will help you stay accountable and consistent in pursuing your passions.

Create a Dedicated Workspace: Designate a space in your home specifically for working on your career goals or personal passions. Having a dedicated workspace can help you stay focused and minimize distractions.

Seek Professional Guidance: If you're pursuing career goals, consider seeking guidance from a career coach or mentor. They can provide valuable insight, advice, and resources to help you navigate your career path.

Develop a Support Network: Connect with like-minded individuals who share your interests or career aspirations. A support network can provide encouragement, advice, and accountability as you work toward your goals.

Utilize Available Resources: Take advantage of online resources, such as webinars, online courses, and podcasts to help you build the skills and knowledge necessary for your career or personal pursuits.

Be Open to New Opportunities: Stay open to opportunities that may come your way, whether it's a networking event, a job opening, or a collaboration. Embrace these opportunities and explore how they can help you advance in your career or personal passions.

Stay Organized: Use tools like planners, to-do lists, and digital apps to keep track of your goals, deadlines, and progress. Staying organized can help you stay focused and motivated as you work toward your aspirations.

Celebrate Your Achievements: Acknowledge and celebrate your progress, no matter how small. Recognizing your achievements can help boost your motivation and self-confidence as you work toward your career goals or personal passions.

The Importance of Purpose and Identity Outside Motherhood

Embracing the importance of finding a sense of purpose and identity outside of motherhood can seem daunting, especially when you're in the thick of parenting. As moms, we're often so consumed by the needs of our children that it's easy to lose sight of our own desires and aspirations. However, rediscovering and nurturing our individuality is a vital component of living a fulfilling and balanced life.

Picture this: it's been a long day of managing tantrums, preparing meals, and tending to your little one's endless demands. You're exhausted, covered in baby food, and yearning for just a moment of peace. But amidst the chaos, you remember that you're not only a mom – you're an artist, an entrepreneur, a fitness enthusiast, or a lover of literature. By holding onto and valuing these unique aspects of your identity, you can reclaim your sense of self and create a more fulfilling life that extends beyond the realm of motherhood.

By cultivating a sense of purpose and identity beyond motherhood, you can experience numerous benefits, including:

Enhanced Self-Esteem: Developing a sense of purpose and identity outside of being a mom can boost your self-esteem and self-worth, as you're able to recognize and appreciate your unique strengths, skills, and accomplishments.

Improved Mental Health: Engaging in activities that bring you personal fulfillment can help reduce stress, anxiety, and feeling overwhelmed. It can also provide a healthy outlet for self-expression, creativity, and personal growth.

Stronger Relationships: Pursuing your interests and passions can help you build connections with like-minded individuals, leading to stronger friendships and support networks. Moreover, having a sense of purpose and identity outside of motherhood can positively impact your relationships with your partner and children, as you're able to bring more balance, happiness, and fulfillment into your home life.

Role Modeling for Children: By pursuing your passions and interests, you demonstrate to your children the importance of personal growth, self-discovery, and resilience. This can encourage them to develop their own interests and sense of purpose as they grow up.

Personal Growth and Development: Engaging in activities that bring you fulfillment and purpose can help you learn new skills, build on existing strengths, and foster personal growth. This can lead to increased confidence, motivation, and a deeper understanding of who you are as an individual.

Greater Life Satisfaction: Finding a sense of purpose and identity outside of motherhood can contribute to overall life satisfaction, as you're able to create a more well-rounded and fulfilling life that encompasses multiple aspects of your identity.

By prioritizing your sense of purpose and identity beyond your role as a mother, you can achieve greater balance, fulfillment, and personal growth. Embrace the unique individual you are and celebrate your passions, interests, and aspirations as you navigate the incredible journey of motherhood.

Are you like Samantha?

Samantha, a mother of two, found herself struggling with her identity after the birth of her second child. Prior to becoming a mom, she had a thriving career as a graphic designer and was passionate about her work. However, after taking time off to care for her children, she felt disconnected from her previous identity and unsure of how to reclaim her sense of purpose. Samantha's story is not unique – many mothers grapple with finding fulfillment outside of their role as caregivers. Despite these challenges, Samantha decided to take action. She began exploring her interests and passions, eventually rediscovering her love for graphic design. Through online courses, networking with other professionals, and setting aside dedicated time for personal projects, Samantha gradually rebuilt her career and sense of self, becoming a beaming light in her household. As a result, her partner was more open with her about his feelings, her children smiled and giggled more often, and Samantha herself went to bed with a happy heart.

Key Takeaways:

- Finding fulfillment and purpose beyond motherhood is essential for personal growth, mental health, and overall well-being.

- Pursuing career goals or personal passions can lead to increased self-esteem, stronger relationships, and a greater sense of life satisfaction.

- Establishing a sense of identity outside of motherhood can benefit not only yourself but also your children, as you model the importance of personal growth, resilience, and self-discovery.

Chapter 5

Modeling Authenticity for Your Children

Get ready to unleash your authentic self and become the ultimate role model for your children. In this chapter, we'll dive into the importance of modeling authenticity and how it positively impacts your child's development. Prepare to embrace your quirks, quirks, and more quirks as we explore the art of being true to yourself while raising children who value authenticity and individuality.

We'll navigate the choppy waters of parenting with a firm belief that staying true to yourself is not only vital for your own well-being but also for your child's growth. We'll explore how mothers can model authenticity and self-care, becoming shining examples for their little ones. So, put on your cape, embrace the chaos, and get ready to shape your children's future by being authentically you—even when you're still in your mismatched pajamas, hair resembling a bird's nest, and your child has decided that now is the perfect time to experiment with finger painting...on the walls.

As you scramble to clean up the chaos, you can't help but wonder how you'll ever teach your child about being true to themselves when your own sanity is hanging on by a thread. When you stay true to who you are, your child learns the importance of self-acceptance and the courage to be themselves. By modeling authenticity, you create a safe space for your child to explore their own identity and develop a strong sense of self. Remember, authenticity is contagious, so let your true colors shine and watch as your child blossoms into a confident, authentic individual.

Let's face it, there will be moments when you feel like a walking contradiction—giving pep talks about self-confidence while secretly wondering if there's any mascara left on your face. Embrace these messy mom moments, laugh at yourself, and remember that imperfections are what make us human. Your children will learn from your ability to embrace your authentic self, flaws and all.

So, dear mom, get ready to unleash your inner superhero. By embracing your authentic self and modeling it for your children, you're not only shaping their future but also creating a world where authenticity reigns supreme. So, put on your invisible crown, kick off those mismatched socks, and let's embark on this adventure of modeling authenticity for your children.

Children Are Sponges

When it comes to raising children, it's easy to get caught up in the endless demands and responsibilities of parenting. We often prioritize their needs above our own, sometimes at the expense of our own identity and well-being. However, it's important to recognize that staying true to oneself can have a profound and positive impact on a child's development.

Children are incredibly perceptive, and they absorb everything that happens around them. They observe our behaviors, attitudes, and actions, even when we don't realize it. By staying true to ourselves, we become powerful role models for our children. They see us living authentically, embracing our passions, and making choices that align with our values. This authenticity creates an environment that encourages them to do the same.

When we stay true to ourselves, we teach our children the importance of self-acceptance and self-expression. They learn that it's okay to be who they truly are and that their unique qualities and interests should be celebrated. By modeling authenticity, we empower our children to develop a strong sense of self and to cultivate their own passions and talents.

Staying true to oneself also allows us to prioritize our own well-being. When we take care of ourselves physically, emotionally, and mentally, we become better equipped to nurture and support our children. By demonstrating self-care practices such as exercise, healthy eating, and self-reflection, we show our children the importance of their own well-being. This sets them up for a lifetime of self-care habits and resilience.

Authenticity also plays a key role in building strong and healthy relationships with our children. When we are true to ourselves, we create an atmosphere of trust and open communication. Our children feel comfortable expressing their thoughts, emotions, and concerns because they know we will listen and validate their experiences. This allows us to guide and support them through life's challenges.

Furthermore, staying true to oneself helps us establish and enforce boundaries within our relationships. By setting clear boundaries and communicating them effectively, we teach our children about consent, respect, and personal autonomy. They learn that it's okay to say no when something doesn't feel right and that their feelings and boundaries should be respected by others. This equips them with essential life skills for healthy relationships in the future.

In addition, modeling authenticity for our children creates a nurturing and supportive family dynamic. It encourages open dialogue, empathy, and understanding within the family. Our children feel safe and secure, knowing that they are accepted for who they are. This fosters their self-esteem and resilience, allowing them to navigate the world with confidence and authenticity.

In the messy moments of motherhood, when exhaustion takes over and self-doubt creeps in, it can be challenging to remember the importance of staying true to ourselves. But by embracing our authentic selves, we not only benefit our own well-being but also shape the future of our children. They learn that it's possible to pursue their dreams, embrace their passions, and live a fulfilling life. They learn that they don't have to sacrifice their true selves for the sake of others.

So, dear mom, remember that you are a shining example for your children. Embrace your authentic self, with all the imperfections and complexities that come with it. Show your children that it's okay to be true to themselves, to follow their hearts, and to live a life that brings them joy and fulfillment. By modeling authenticity, you are giving your children the greatest gift of all - the courage to be themselves.

How to Model Authenticity and Self-Care for Your Children

As mothers, we have the power to shape our children's perception of authenticity and self-care through our daily actions and behaviors. Here are some examples of how we can model authenticity and self-care for our children:

Expressing Emotions: Show your children that it's okay to feel and express a range of emotions. Be open and honest about your feelings, whether it's joy, frustration, or sadness. By doing so, you teach them the importance of acknowledging and processing their emotions in a healthy way.

Prioritizing Self-Care: Make self-care a non-negotiable part of your routine, and involve your children in the process. Let them see you engage in activities that bring you joy and relaxation or allow them to wait while you wash your face and put on your makeup. Explain to them that taking care of yourself allows you to be a better mom and person.

Setting Boundaries: Teach your children about boundaries by setting and enforcing them in your own life. Let them see you say no to things that don't align with your values or priorities. Show them that setting boundaries is essential for self-respect and maintaining a healthy balance in life.

Pursuing Personal Interests: Share your passions and hobbies with your children. Let them see you engage in activities that bring you fulfillment and make you come alive. This could be painting, playing a musical instrument, or practicing a sport. Encourage them to explore their own interests and support them in pursuing their passions.

Honoring Your Values: Live your life in alignment with your values and demonstrate the importance of integrity. Explain to your children the reasons behind your choices and actions, and let them witness how your values guide your decisions. Encourage them to develop their own set of values and to stand up for what they believe in.

Practicing Self-Compassion: Show your children that it's okay to make mistakes and to be kind to oneself. When you have a challenging day or make a parenting blunder, practice self-compassion and model self-forgiveness. Talk to them about the importance of being gentle with oneself and learning from mistakes.

Celebrating Individuality: Embrace and celebrate your unique qualities and encourage your children to do the same. Teach them that diversity and individuality are strengths to be cherished. Help them recognize and appreciate the differences in themselves and others, fostering a culture of acceptance and inclusivity.

Effective Communication: Model open and honest communication with your children and within your family. Encourage dialogue, active listening, and empathy. Show them how to express their thoughts and emotions constructively, and guide them in resolving conflicts peacefully.

Remember, authenticity and self-care are lifelong journeys, and we may stumble along the way. But by consistently demonstrating these values and behaviors, we provide our children with a strong foundation for embracing their own authentic selves and prioritizing their well-being.

Are you like Emma?

Emma, a mother of two, always prioritized authenticity and individuality in her parenting approach. She encouraged her children, Lily and Ethan, to embrace their unique qualities and follow their passions. Emma noticed that Lily, at a young age, had a deep love for dancing and expressing herself through this kind of art form. She provided Lily with a playlist of upbeat music and encouraged her to explore her creativity without judgment. Lily's confidence in her dancing abilities grew, and she began choreographing dance routines, showcasing her art form in front of friends and family members when they came to visit.

Studies have shown that children who are encouraged to be authentic and express their true selves have higher self-esteem, better emotional well-being, and experience less psychological distress compared to children who feel pressured to conform to societal expectations. They also found that authentic children were more likely to develop positive relationships, engage in prosocial behavior, and demonstrate higher levels of academic achievement.

Studies also show that most teens believe that being authentic and true to oneself is important for their overall happiness and well-being, and adolescents who embrace their authentic selves are less likely to engage in risky behaviors such as substance abuse and delinquency. It has been reported that employees who feel their authentic selves were welcomed and valued in the workplace and experience higher levels of job satisfaction, engagement, and productivity.

These stories and statistics highlight the significant impact that embracing authenticity and individuality can have on a child's development and overall well-being. Encouraging children to be true to themselves sets the foundation for a fulfilling and meaningful life journey.

Key Takeaways:

- Staying true to oneself positively impacts a child's development:
- Mothers can model authenticity and self-care for their children by prioritizing our own well-being:
- Raising children who value authenticity and individuality is crucial to fostering their self-confidence, creativity, and resilience.
- Children who grow up embracing their authenticity, are more likely to form genuine and meaningful connections with others.

Chapter 6

Overcoming Guilt and Shame

Let's face it, guilt and shame seem to be constant companions on the journey of motherhood. "I forgot to pack my child's hat for school." Guilt! "My toddler isn't speaking full sentences yet." Shame! The amount of daily bullying I do to myself somedays makes me think, *No wonder I can't put a smile on my face.* But what if I told you there's a way to break free from their grip and embrace a life filled with self-compassion and self-forgiveness?

Whether it's the guilt of taking time for yourself, feeling like you're not doing enough, or comparing yourself to other moms, we've all been there.

Picture this: It's the end of a long and chaotic day. You've been running on little sleep, juggling endless tasks, and trying to keep up with the demands of motherhood. You finally manage to put your little one down for a nap, and in that precious moment of quiet, you decide to treat yourself to a hot cup of coffee. But as you reach for the mug, you accidentally knock it over, spilling coffee all over the kitchen counter. In that instant, frustration wells up inside you, and you can't help but berate yourself for being so clumsy. The voice of guilt starts whispering in your ear, telling you that you're not doing enough, that you're a failure.

This messy mom moment may seem trivial, but it's a perfect example of how guilt can seep into our daily lives and weigh us down. It's moments like these when we question our abilities, compare ourselves to others, and doubt our worth as mothers. We may feel guilty for taking a moment for ourselves, for making mistakes, or for not meeting the impossible standards we've set for ourselves.

But here's the truth: you're not alone. Every mother has her fair share of spills, mishaps, and moments of self-doubt. It's part of the beautiful mess that is motherhood. Especially when you can look back and laugh at how trivial it was in the first place. And it's in these moments that we have the opportunity to practice self-compassion, to forgive ourselves for being human, and to embrace the imperfect journey we're on.

So, the next time you find yourself in a messy mom moment, remember that it's just a fleeting moment in time. Shake it off, pour yourself another cup, forget about the never-ending tasks on your to do list and embrace it, learn from it, and let go.

This Is Normal

Guilt and shame are two emotions that often accompany the journey of motherhood. As a new mom, you may find yourself grappling with these feelings, questioning your choices, and doubting your abilities. It's important to recognize that these emotions are common and experienced by many mothers. Let's take a closer look at the common feelings of guilt and shame that new mothers face:

Guilt Over Self-Care: One of the most prevalent sources of guilt for new moms is taking time for self-care. You may feel guilty for prioritizing your own needs, whether it's going for a walk alone, indulging in a hobby, or simply taking a break. Society often places an expectation on mothers to be selfless and constantly available for their children. This can lead to guilt when you engage in activities that are solely for your own well-being.

Guilt Over Work-Life Balance: Balancing motherhood with work commitments can be challenging. Many moms feel guilty for pursuing their career goals or for needing to work outside the home. This guilt can stem from the fear of not being fully present for your child or feeling like you're not meeting societal expectations of what a "good" mom should do.

Guilt Over Not Meeting Expectations: As a new mom, you may set high expectations for yourself, striving to be the perfect parent. When things don't go as planned or you make mistakes, guilt can creep in. Whether it's missing a milestone, struggling with breastfeeding, or feeling overwhelmed, these moments can trigger feelings of guilt and self-doubt.

Shame Over Perceived Inadequacy: New mothers often compare themselves to others and may feel shame when they believe they're not measuring up to the standards set by society or other moms. This can include feeling shame for not having a perfectly organized home, not looking a certain way, or not having all the answers when it comes to parenting.

Shame Over Needing Help: Asking for help or seeking support is a sign of strength, but many new moms feel ashamed or inadequate when they can't do it all on their own. Whether it's hiring a babysitter, leaning on family and friends, or reaching out to a support group, the shame of needing assistance can be a significant barrier to self-care and well-being.

It's important to remember that these feelings of guilt and shame are not a reflection of your worth as a mother. They are normal responses to the challenges and pressures of motherhood. By acknowledging and addressing these emotions, you can begin to let go of the guilt and shame and focus on building a healthier and more compassionate relationship with yourself.

Strategies for Overcoming These Feelings and Embracing One's True Self

Let's dive deeper into strategies for overcoming feelings of guilt and shame and embracing your true self as a mother:

Practice Self-Compassion: It's important to be kind and understanding towards yourself. Acknowledge that being a mom is a learning process and that mistakes are a natural part of the journey. Treat yourself with the same compassion and forgiveness you would extend to a friend (or your toddler!) Remind yourself that you're doing the best you can and that it's okay to make mistakes.

Challenge Unrealistic Expectations: Reflect on the expectations you have placed on yourself as a mother. Are they realistic and attainable? Recognize that perfection is unattainable, and it's okay to have moments of imperfection. Set realistic goals and standards for yourself, focusing on what truly matters and letting go of unnecessary pressures.

Reframe Negative Self-Talk: Pay attention to your inner dialogue and challenge negative self-talk. Replace self-critical thoughts with positive affirmations and reminders of your strengths and accomplishments. Remember that you are a capable and loving mother, doing your best to provide for your child's needs.

Let Go of Comparisons: Avoid comparing yourself to other moms or societal standards. Life is hard enough without social media standards and comparisons being rubbed in our faces. Each mother and child have unique experiences and challenges. Focus on your own journey and celebrate your individual strengths and successes.

Embrace Imperfection and Flexibility: Accept that motherhood is a journey filled with ups and downs. Embrace the imperfections and allow yourself to adapt and learn along the way. Give yourself permission to make mistakes and grow from them.

It seems like such a misconception these days that in order to be a good mom you have to do everything for your child, your entire day should revolve around them, and your entire social calendar should include them. The mom-guilt of not doing enough, taking them to enough places, and buying them enough toys can be intense. Take this as a gentle reminder that it's okay if your child is four and hasn't been to the zoo. You'll get there one day! If you don't have time to take your child for ice cream, don't be hard on yourself; they have their entire life to eat too much sugar. If you're tired, feeling sick, or hate the weather outside, it's okay to keep them indoors playing or watching TV here and there because downtime is good for them, too. I often think of my childhood and remind myself that my mom didn't have me in sports every night, and I sure wasn't at different play centers every weekend, and my bedroom was not full of toys, but I never look back and think to myself, "*I wish I got all that.*" In fact, just the opposite – I'm happy I wasn't carted around to obligations every night or weekend. Research shows that boredom fosters creativity in our kids! The guilt mothers put on themselves in this era to always do and provide is not realistic nor fair to ourselves, and it's important to let those false expectations go. In my life in general, I like to remind myself of the saying, "Less is more." I truly believe that in certain aspects, this applies to motherhood and raising our children as well.

By implementing these strategies, you can gradually overcome feelings of guilt and shame and embrace your true self as a mother. Remember that you are enough, and your love and presence in your child's life are invaluable. Let go of the guilt and shame that hold you back and step into your power as an authentic and confident mother and embrace a future filled with love, growth, and acceptance.

Are you like Lisa?

Lisa often found herself overwhelmed with feelings of guilt and shame. She constantly questioned her parenting decisions, doubting her ability to meet the ever-increasing demands of motherhood. Lisa carried the weight of guilt for not being able to do it all, for not having endless reserves of patience and energy, and for feeling like she was falling short in some areas of her children's lives. These feelings of guilt and shame affected her self-esteem, leaving her feeling unworthy and inadequate as a mother.

One day, while she watched her children playing outside with complete enjoyment, she realized that her children clearly did not think this little of her and her parenting skills. Amongst their giggles in the background of her crowded inner thoughts, it dawned on her that all the guilt and shame she held inside was merely from ideas that she created in her own head, and it was hindering her from being fully present in her children's activities. She, as a mother, was doing the best she could. That was all her children needed.

Conclusion

isten up, moms! This book has been all about one thing: empowering you to stay true to yourself while rocking the mom life. We've tackled the challenges, the guilt, the juggling act, and everything in between. The main idea that has been at the core of our journey together is this: you can be an incredible mom without losing sight of the amazing, unique individual you've always been.

Motherhood is a rollercoaster ride, no doubt about it. It's filled with joy, love, and yes, even messy moments that make you question your sanity. But amidst all the chaos, it's crucial to remember that you are more than just a mom. You have passions, dreams, and goals that deserve to be nurtured alongside your little one.

Throughout this book, we've explored practical strategies for maintaining your sense of self, pursuing personal fulfillment, and embracing authenticity. We've delved into the challenges of finding balance, navigating relationships, and overcoming guilt and shame. We've discussed the importance of self-care, setting boundaries, and creating a support network. And let's not forget the power of modeling authenticity for your children and raising them to value their own uniqueness.

So, here's the bottom line, mama: you matter. Your dreams matter. Your identity matters. By prioritizing yourself, taking care of your needs, and embracing who you truly are, you are not only enriching your own life but also setting a powerful example for your children.

Remember, there will be days when you feel like you're barely holding it together. That's okay. I'm sure you had those days before becoming a mom too. Embrace the messy moments, learn from the challenges, and give yourself permission to grow and evolve. And never forget to surround yourself with a tribe of other amazing moms who understand the struggles, the triumphs, and everything in between.

As we conclude this journey together, I want you to hold onto this truth: you have what it takes to be an extraordinary mom and an extraordinary woman. Embrace your uniqueness, pursue your passions, and always strive to be true to yourself. The world needs more moms like you – fierce, authentic, and unstoppable.

So go out there, mama, and continue to rock the mom life with unwavering love, boundless strength, and an unapologetic sense of self. You've got this, and I'm cheering you on every step of the way. Remember, you are a superhero in disguise, and the world is a better place because of you. Keep shining, keep thriving, and never forget the incredible woman that you are!

About the Author

Maggie Dee is a new mom, writer, and advocate for helping women maintain their identity and personal growth while navigating motherhood. After experiencing firsthand the challenges of adjusting to life as a new mom, Maggie was determined to empower other women to embrace their individuality and passions without sacrificing their role as a caregiver.

Maggie's writing is rooted in her personal experiences and shares practical strategies and inspiration for women to reclaim their sense of self and continue pursuing their goals and aspirations as they navigate the complexities of motherhood. Her compassionate and relatable voice resonates with women at all stages of their parenting journey, from those considering starting a family to seasoned moms looking for guidance and support.

With a background in psychology and a passion for helping others, Maggie's mission is to empower women to thrive as individuals and as mothers. She is a regular contributor to various online publications where she shares her insights and advice on motherhood, self-care, and personal development.

As a new mom herself, Maggie understands the unique challenges that come with balancing motherhood and personal growth. Her writing is a testament to the power of perseverance and self-discovery, encouraging women to prioritize their well-being and passions while embracing the joys and responsibilities of motherhood.